AIX-EN-PROVENCE
A STROLL THROUGH TIME

AIX-EN-PROVENCE

A STROLL THROUGH TIME

Photography by Patrick Chevalier
Text by Amos Booth

EDISUD
La Calade, 13090 Aix-en-Provence
France

ISBN 2-85744-351-X

Published in France.

LA PLACE DES PRÊCHEURS

"IT hath a monstrous beauty, like the hind quarters of an elephant." The *Palais de Justice* (Courts of Law), upstart "wedding cake in an antique shop," stands square, brash, and unblushing, among its more venerable neighbors. It has about it a touch of bravado, like an Eiffel Tower, Beaubourg, or a *Pyramide du Louvre*. From without, it is a marvel of incongruity, solemn, smug, and "purpose built." From within, a universe of light and shadow, entire unto itself, of cool lofty classicism.

1

To view the higher-browed but lower elevated fronts on the opposing side of the square, you must stand on the monumental steps of the *Palais* itself, lest, seeing from another angle, the eye be distracted by the "fearful symmetry" and solemn, voluminous rectitude of the 19th century. Behind those massive doors sits the High Court of Appeals. The building is a statement. Questions belong within.

The Palace of the Counts of Provence stood here for six centuries, until 1775. It was the home of *Parlement,* one of the region's three "scourges," and of the *Cour des Comptes* (Tax Office), which, for those who paid presumably came in a "close fourth." For Aix it was a blessing and a sinecure.

Despite the marauding *"pastoureaux"* (Crusaders who didn't quite make it, either there, or back), the Black Death, and the Hundred Years' War, the *Place des Prêcheurs* has a fond, if imperfect, memory of a time when it was the heart of a capital city. The *Via Aurelia* arrived here from Rome ; a mausoleum and two Roman towers marked the entrance to the *Colonia Julia Augusta Aquis Sextiis*, which is how the Romans pronounced Aix. The towers were linked with great stone walls, and within them the Counts of Provence created "the most refined court in Europe."

It was here, in the capital of Provence that "love was invented in the 13th and 14th centuries," or so taught Paul Chovelon to generations of American students who noted the fact carefully, only smiling their disbelief.

Oh, sublime fib, a Provençal truth. It is Panisse's deathbed confession : "Dying doesn't bother me. But I'm so sad to leave this life." It is the endless joking and jousting of the "folk from the *Palais"* and their Dominican neighbors from the convent of the *Prêcheurs*, catty corner across the *Place*. (Neither party was renowned for being taciturn). And it is Marguerite du Périer : *Rose elle a vécu, ce que vivent les roses, l'espace d'un matin* (Rose she lived, what roses live, a morning's moment) far surpassing in celebrity her most illustrious family who lived at N° 1, *Place des Prêcheurs*. (One of her descendants, invented the fireman's pump). What does it matter that her name was Marguerite, not Rose ? Provençal folk know both fact and fiction. Fact makes them smile.

But we anticipate. The King's garden, where René d'Anjou, *Comte de Provence, Roi de Jérusalem et des deux Siciles* strolled among his "carnations, roses, mace, and all kinds of flowers," like Daudet's good Pope among his vines, stood here, outside the Palace walls. What if, after all, his garden was but a vegetable patch, with "cabbage, beans, spinach, borage, parsley, onions, garlic, and leeks ?" Does that mean that the King does not today rejoice from 8am to 12.30pm on Tuesdays, Thursdays, and Saturdays when, on market days, this same land is surrendered 500 years later to the merchants selling the distant progeny of the plants that he cultivated ? It is, he might say, an improvement upon the gruesome entertainment of the scaffold which, until 1775, reigned in the center of the square. Its presence there contributed handsomely to the popularity of the *Cours* as "a pleasant place to stroll." The troubadours left. The Courts of Love were deserted, and Courts of Law took their place. In 1481 Provence joined France "not as a subaltern, but as an equal" and in 1501 *Parlement* arrived. The squabble between license and censure is sublime and ongoing : "Nobody was sure that he would not one day fall madly in love with somebody who was completely indifferent to him ! What delight !.. That's when you arrived with your public prosecutor husband." Then, as Giraudoux tells it, "love died in Aix," but we know that it was an ephemeral death.

Aix has long hesitated about where its heart is. That roaming fickle organ has suffered many transplants, only some of which have left visible trace. Once, doubtless, it was a Roman forum ; once, perhaps, in the *Ville des Tours*, near the *Cours des Minimes* ; and who doubts the claims of the *Place de la Mairie*, or the *Cours Mirabeau* ? But, even today, half a millennium after the good King René, every Aixois who passes through the ancient archways of the *Passage Agard* or the *rue Rifle Rafle*, between 8am and 12.30pm on Tuesdays, Thursdays, and Saturdays and enters the King's garden, knows precisely where it is - here among the chatter of the merchants, presiding over the King's "cabbage, beans, spinach, borage, parsley, onions, garlic and leeks."

2

3

4

6

7

8

9

10

11

12

THE CITY OF THE COUNTS AND SAINT-SAUVEUR

"Aix. Un aveugle croit qu'il pleut." Jean Cocteau.
("Aix. A blind man thinks it is raining.")

AN Aixois will tell you that water flows uphill. It thrusts its way up through earth and stone until it finds a pipe stuck between the teeth of a cherub, a lion, a dolphin, or one of those hideous carved heads that would discourage a gargoyle. It then falls, splashing into a basin, and for our pleasure, repeats itself. But truth compels the suspicion that the Aixois lie, and that Cocteau's blind man knew more about Aix than Cocteau did. Splashing water in Aix can, and often does, mean rain. I call to witness this month of May, 1988 and its damp forerunner, the month of April, and many a June that has the Aixois shaking his head : "Pourri" (rotted). The judgment is final. Worse than dead.

To our July music festival-goer, however, this is right nonsense, the craven wailing of a people demanding, but not deserving, sympathy. To human knowledge, *Aix sous la pluie* (Aix in the rain) has never existed. No illustrated brochure vaunting the city's charms shows sky but of the purest azure. Cézanne painted in the sun, and the *Ville d'Eaux* trumpeted by road signs as we approach the city by autoroute refers, of course, to the springs that, even before the Romans, decided that this would be a choice spot to build an *Hôtel des Thermes*. Cocteau's blind man must have been standing in the *Place d'Albertas*. No other fountain in Aix splashes so eloquently like a heavy shower on an empty street. No other square is so perfect, quiet in its perfection, at peace with itself and with its own, 18th century. It is a rhythmic blending of arched windows, shutters, wrought iron balconies, punctuated by Ionic pilasters, and impudent *mascarons*, those disembodied stone heads that stand guard over doors and windows, lest unwelcome visitors or spirits make to enter. It is Mozart in stone, as limpid and moving as a Figaro, a Don Giovanni, or a Papageno strutting on the stage of the Archibishop's Palace up the street. And when darkness falls and the "stage lights" of the *Place d'Albertas* go on, shabby and faded forms and colors are transfigured and the shadows rise in song.

Opposite, on the other side of the *rue Espariat* the *Hôtel d'Albertas*, in a different but no less pleasing mode, exemplifies an earlier, more sumptuous style. When its doors swing open, the garden courtyard, fountain, trees, orangeries, and the majestic stairway reveal a brief vision of idyllic seclusion unsuspected by passers-by in the *rue Aude*, a few feet away.

Between the *Place d'Albertas* and the *Place de l'Hôtel de Ville* lies a dense thicket of history. Time criss-crosses over intertwined styles, functions, status. This is the sixteenth, seventeenth and eighteenth centuries, but lurking are the *Ville des Comtes*, and the Roman colony.

In our century the merchants have taken over the street-vaulted level. Even the 16th century Hôtel Peyroneti (N° 13, rue Aude) with its vermiculated stone and its barrel-vaulted hallway is home to a wine merchant. By its date, 1562, and its style it is unique ; the Renaissance in Aix. It has, too, historical and literary resonances, since Bienvenu de Miollis was born here in 1753 and his brother, Sextius, in 1759. Armed with such names it is not surprising that the former who became Bishop of Digne was Victor Hugo's model for Bishop Bienvenu Myriel in *Les Misérables*, while Sextius, whose name recalls

Aix's founder, Caius Sextius Calvinus, fought under Rochambeau at Yorktown.

The *rue Aude* leads to the *rue Maréchal-Foch*, and to Aix's second market place, the *Place Richelme*. Unlike the *grand marché* it is open every morning, and specializes in local produce. The Aixois still refer to it as *derrière la Poste* (behind the Post Office), but to be truthful, the Post Office occupies but a part of that immense building which deserves to rank as the world's handsomest barn. It was built in 1759 as a storage silo for the grain taxes, collected in kind at the *Porte Saint-Jean* and deposited here in safe sight of the *Hôtel de Ville*. Neither barns nor tax offices enjoy such architectural distinction these days. The façade which faces the *Place de l'Hôtel de Ville* is a beautifully modulated and harmonious ensemble, perhaps in contrast to the discordant moans of the tax payers themselves. On the pediment the sculptor Chastel has left much to ponder : a bored and bearded Rhône reclines against a spilling urn (is he ordering another drink ?) while the Durance, momentarily disguised as Cybele, prepares to climb out of the conjugal bed. A cornucopia gives a broad hint to tax payers just what is expected of them and their land, the sun streams stone rays upon all, and a leopard, (why a leopard in Provence ?) lies nearby, watchfully. Cybele's foot, and a fair portion of her leg, is poised in mid-air for us to admire. Has she not been told that the floor is thirty feet below ? One suspects that she is about to run off with a less waterlogged companion. Plans to divert the waters of the Durance in order to irrigate Provence go back at least to the sixteenth century and it was not until the middle of the 20th century, when she eloped with the Canal de Provence, that the Durance did, in fact, desert her bed. Only wide tracts of

14

15

16

PLACE
D'ALBERTAS

stones with a narrow stream meandering in their midst bear witness. But, thanks to her promiscuity, the cornucopia has been filled, and it has spilled into the market places of Provence and Europe.

In front of the *Halle aux Grains* is Aix's flower market, a riot of colors and scents. This is the *Place de l'Hôtel de Ville* which came into being in 1741. Until then the City Hall itself had been crowded into anonymity by the *rue Droite* which passed in front of it, depriving Aix of the view of one of its loveliest buildings. The ornate façade, the wrought iron rays above the gates, spread like a peacock's pride, and the courtyard leading to the ceremonial stairway, all in the soft pastel *pierre de Rognes* (Rognes stone) make of Aix's civic architecture its civic pride. On the first floor to the left is one of France's most prestigious library collections, the *Bibliothèque Méjanes*, and to the right, on ground level, the vaulted *Salle des Mariages* with the splendid *Salle des Etats* above it.

19

VENTS
DU SUD

MIEL

25

26

27

TIQUITÉ
JOUR
miniclaire

29

30

32

LE BOURG SAINT-SAUVEUR

THROUGH the belfry is another world, the *Bourg Saint-Sauveur*. We are in the Roman Castrum, discreetly announced by the large cut stones at the base of the belfry tower and of the corner houses of the *rue Gaston de Saporta*. The cathedral, a few paces up the street, spans almost two millennia. Some stones and columns have changed allegiance, but not place, for they were there with the Romans, and todaythey are with us. The crown arrived on the tower during the last years of the 19th century. Yet, despite its many ages and styles, *Saint-Sauveur* lives as one. Do not waste time on those dispiriting shutters that hide the "real" early 16th century doors sculpted by Jean Guiramand. Bribe the sexton and he will open them. Bribe him again and he will show you the "good" King René painted in 1476, but surely not flattered by his favorite artist Nicolas Froment. The King, whose reputation in this part of town is somewhat tarnished, is kneeling before the burning bush. His second wife, Jeanne de Laval (she is "43 and was never pretty") is facing him. The King himself who was 67 at the time was not conspicuously pretty either. The bush, however, is attractive. It represents the mystery of the virginity of Mary which "burns, but remains green."

Brave the sexton's frown, for he cannot charge you for this, and penetrate behind the high altar. There in *Saint-Mitre*'s Chapel you will stand on a tomb. This is not the saint's but that of Nicolai, Archbishop of Avignon. Facing you, however, is the saint's portrait, of doubtful likeness for it was painted in 1480. Scenes from *Saint-Mitre*'s life, like cartoons, are portrayed on the same panel. The unfortunate has been beheaded and he is holding his head in his hands. His gesture bespeaks divine intervention. Legend says that "when he arose to pick up his head the good people shrank back in horror and the Roman soldiers split their sides laughing." Legend also says that he "kissed his head," but this is not portrayed.

Never mind legend. A more exciting truth speaks here, for it shows us Aix in the 15th century, with the cathedral tower and the palaces, oh the palaces, of the time of King René ! If this is the *Bourg Saint-Sauveur*, allow us a sigh for the *Palais des Comtes* !

Here we must leave the king, the saint, the piece of Roman forum thoughtfully bared for us in the romanesque nave, the 4th century baptistery and this glorious *macédoine* of styles and ages. We will spend a moment in the cloister. Though Aix's heart may roam, in repose since the 12th century its soul is here.

34

35

36

38

39

40

41

42

TABAC

44

45

48

49

50

51

54

LE COURS

"THE only people you see working on the *Cours* are the Telamones who are holding up the balcony over the door of the *Hôtel de Maurel de Pontevès.*" So say the local wags, but this is unfair, slightly libelous even. The balcony that causes those massive muscles to bulge and those male features to contort with pain is a light and delicate thing, a tray that any smiling female caryatid would bear aloft without a ripple of her comely limbs.

But there they stand, or "surge" rather for they emerge from the stone portals themselves, lending a touch of wit to the grace and solemnity of N° 38 *Cours Mirabeau*, and to the imposing row of 17th century mansions that, on either side, marks the northern boundary of the *Quartier Mazarin.* Like its neighbors, N° 38 is always in the shade, or so it seems, until one ventures down the side streets to discover the sun-drenched gardens, the fountains, the coach houses, and the servants' quarters that lie behind those imposing façades.

Today it is the banks, the most exquisite and expensive *pâtissiers* in town, and the so-called "liberal" professions that have taken possession of this "shady" side of the *Cours*. Opposite, in almost undivided throng, café upon café spills out onto the broad sunny sidewalk, establishing for anyone who cares about such matters, the undisputed *"supériorité de l'homme assis."* Here politics, intrigue, and the world order are redeemed, reputations undone (they are done elswhere), and the original vocation of the *Cours* pursued diligently : to see and to be seen. Two decrees, 1649 and 1651, had ordained that the old ramparts, lists, and ditches that bordered the meadows of the archbishop's palace be replaced by a "carriage-way which would serve the public, without, for any reason whatsoever, changing its original intent." That straight line, 220 fathoms long and 21 fathoms wide (about 440 meters by 42), still challenges the labyrinthine mental processes of our 20th century Aixois. For Giraudoux "half the distance they cover in their daily journeying is dedicated to love." As though an entire population were rehearsing illicit passions in obedience to some higher law that disputes with Justice, over the soul of its inhabitants.

Just off center, on the site of an old water-mill, at the "top" of the *Cours*, stands the *Hôtel du Poët*, commanding a view of the broad highway that leads us to the *fontaine de la Rotonde.* Like the reredos of a great cathedral it faces the setting sun, towering above the "priest" on its altar steps, the good King René, of whom only the best is thought and said. Since it was surely he who introduced the muscat grape into Provence, he is holding a branch in his left hand as evidence. And on either side of the "nave," magnificent plane trees reach to the firmament with their arching branches. At the "west end," before the rose of the setting sun, stands the grand font, Aix's most ostentatious 19th century water works, surmounted by its three Graces, not Aglaia, Euphrosyne, and Thalia, but Agriculture, the Arts, and Justice. In deference to the city's long and distinguished tradition as the seat of a *parlement* (High Court), and the role played by its Law Courts and, more recently, its Law Faculty, it is Justice who faces Aix, while her less favored sister, Agriculture, and the Arts face toward Marseille and Avignon.

Down the middle of the *Cours*, decorative reminders of Aix's origins and its name (Aix means "water"), stand four fountains, the best known of which is remarkable for its rusticity. It is a simple moss-covered rock whose warm waters have been diverted from the Roman thermal springs at the *Place des Bagniers*. The *fontaine d'eau chaude* once sported four stone figures, children holding a basin into which splashed the steaming water that still exudes cheer, solace, and warmth on many a frosty Provençal night.
The *Cours* is a place for all seasons, a worldly refuge from the parish churches, convents, and cloisters that once dominated *le vieil Aix*. It goes late to bed and rises early. Its students, musicians, sword swallowers, trinket vendors, buskers, artists, writers, philosophers, poets, lawyers, mountebanks, rich men, poor men, beggarmen, bourgeois, they're all there, young and old, watching the pageant, playing their part. They are the pageant, too.
But, if you want to see the *Cours* at its best, come early on a spring or summer morning. The sunlight is beginning to filter through the leaves. Shafts of light break through the soft shadows, and the havoc of our 20th century carriages is momentarily suspended. Man has withdrawn his noisome presence, yielding his place to the dawn chorus, and the magic of the empty stage stands in hushed anticipation. It is a high moment in the noble conspiracy of nature, art, and the gods.

56

57

58

59

60

61

62

63

64

65

66

67

72 73 74 75

76

THE QUARTIER MAZARIN

MICHEL MAZARIN, Archbishop of Aix and brother of Giulio, the Cardinal, had a sure grasp of politics and things temporal. He has left his mark less, perhaps, on the soul of his people than on their real estate. In 1646, by letters patent from the King, he was authorized to enclose in the city of Aix "all of this new neighborhood, including the parish of *Saint Jean*, and the gardens and meadows belonging to the Archdiocese lying to the south of the ramparts."

Few parts have remained so untouched, timelocked, and tranquil. This was "urban planning" on a scale that Aix had not known for centuries. The city increased in area by one third, making of the new *Cours* an ample bisector "where once lay a mere tangent."

The *Quartier Mazarin* was no low cost housing development for artisans and workers. It was "by the rich and for the rich" and for an ascending class who were thronging the tribunals, serving in the high ranks of the army, or following in the train of a *prince magnifique*, the *Comte d'Alais*, Governor of Provence. The historian, de Haitze, muses : "Who would have imagined that vanity would one day be lodged as a person ?" The century of Descartes drew straight lines, and knew about geometry. With the church of *Saint-Jean-de-Malte* at one end and the *Porte des Augustins* at the other, the new city wall was slung to the south like the bow to its taut string stretched along the *Cours*. The land was criss-crossed with streets, intersecting at right angles and affording vistas uninterrupted and unique in Aix.

Almost dead center in the *Quartier Mazarin* stands the *Place des Quatre Dauphins*. The dolphins are balancing gracefully on their chins, spouting of course, but spouting gracefully, more gracefully than would have spouted the Archbishop's brother whose statue, *en pied*, had originally been planned for the site. "With this fountain the social and legal fabric of Aix affixed its seal to the square," writes Monsieur Bouyala d'Arnaud. And so it is, with its most lovely view down the *rue Cardinale* of the front of the church of *Saint Jean*.

Residental areas are home to their residents. To the stranger, they are handsome, but closed, doors, drawn curtains, gardens that are private, turned inwards, and façades, not faces. They are the mask.

To enter is to retreat three hundred years. The great door closes heavily, the past assails the nostrils as the eyes adjust to the darkness and to the monumental scale of an entrance hall, whose grand staircase is enclosed by its wrought-iron balustrade. High ceilings with their plaster mouldings *(gypseries)*, mythology in paint, baroque, *trompe-l'œil* panels, tall doors capped by medallions, long curtains, high windows fastened with espagnolettes, even an indoor fountain, they scarcely breathe their faded splendor. Since they arrived delivered by the hand of a Daret, Chastel, Toro, or Pierre Puget, they have not stirred.

The *Quartier Mazarin* is "zoned" territory, as heavily defended as Park Avenue. Nevertheless commerce has infiltrated the *rue Frédéric-Mistral*, the *rue du Quatre-Septembre*, and parallel streets, seeping down from the *Cours*. Near the church of *Saint-Jean-de-Malte* it is abundant, for the *rue d'Italie*

(Via Aurelia) is one of Aix's oldest streets, and Aix makes its living by selling.

Long before Michel Mazarin, the knights of St. John of Jerusalem established a chapel and shelter next to the *Via Aurelia*, on its south side, about three hundrd yards short of the city gate. With their hostelry opening onto the high-road they must have been a reassuring sight to travellers arriving after nightfall. In 1275 they built their church with its spire and turrets, a nice compromise between temporal and spiritual imperatives, a toned down Provençal brand of Gothic with a touch of the militant.

Two of Provence's most distinguished Counts, Alphonse II and Raimond Béranger V, are buried here. Both are remembered for their women folk. The former married Garsende de Sabran in 1209, thereby uniting the house of Barcelona to that of Forcalquier. Alphonse protected poets and troubadours at a time when there was cause for song and need for protection. Raimond Bérenger, his son, married off his four daughters in what has been described as a *"feu d'artifice"* (firework display), Marguerite to Louis IX (Saint Louis, no less), Eleonore to Henry III of England, Sanche to the Duke of Cornwall, and Beatrice to Charles I of Anjou (King of Sicily, Count of Provence and brother of Louis IX). Everyone in Aix wanted to be buried at *Saint-Jean-de-Malte* after that, and the cathedral *Saint Sauveur* had to fight back bravely for its dead, finally settling for a tax on those who preferred *Saint Jean*.

Do not leave the *Quartier Mazarin* without visiting the house of the Commander of the Order of the Knights of St. John, for here is the *Musée Granet*, rich, but richly overshadowed by its *"grand absent,"* Cézanne. Some watercolors are here

79

80

to remind us, ruefully, of Aix's most prodigious gift... to the world.

But here, too, is a strong voice in stone telling of Aix's origins on the hill, hard by the *route de Puyricard*. The heads, torsos, prancing horse, hand on skull, are fragments from pre-Roman "Entremont," whose ramparts, streets, and walls mount their watch across to the *Chaîne de l'Etoile*, the *Sainte-Baume* and the *Etang de Berre*. For two thousand four hundred years the "Aixois" has been building with stone, and cutting it into strange and beautiful shapes. It must be his likeness and legacy, like the *Quartier Mazarin*.

HOTEL
CAR
DINAL

84

85

86

87

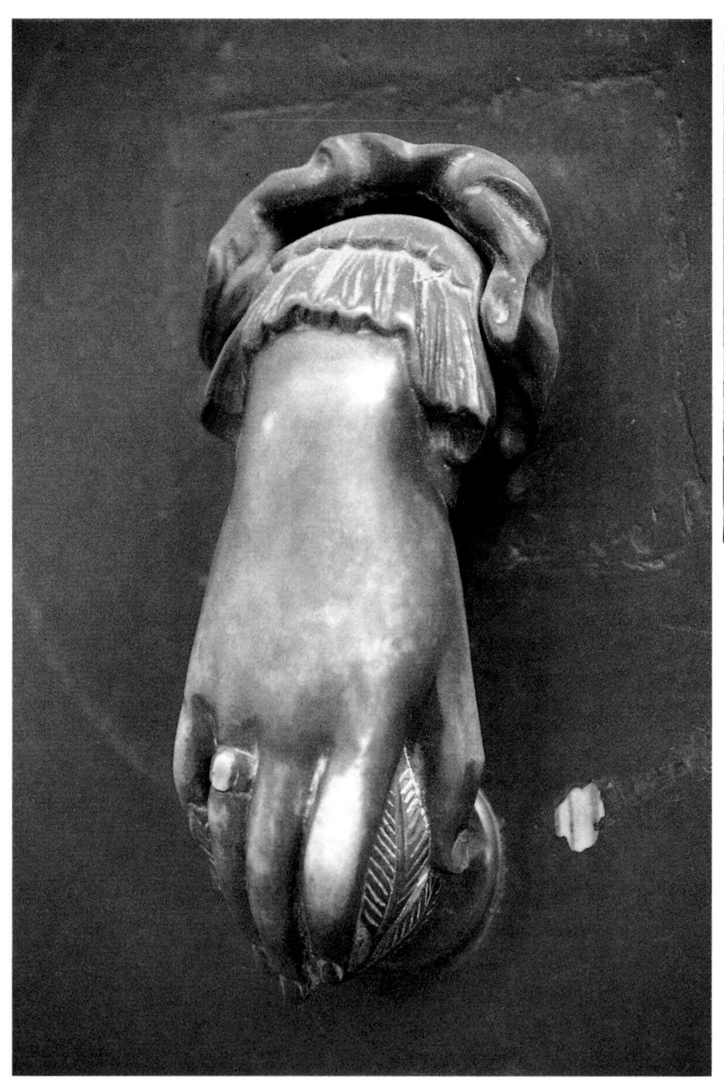

88

89

THE PAVILLON VENDÔME

LOUIS DE MERCŒUR, Duke of Vendôme, Governor of Provence, Cardinal, grandson of Henri VI and Gabrielle d'Estrées, was to have built his palace on the *Cours*. He was given 20.000 *livres* for the purpose. His wife, Mazarin's niece, Laure de Mancini, had died, and he had fallen in love with Lucrèce de Rascas, née Forbin Soliès, widow of a certain Honoré de Rascas. She is known as *"la Belle du Carnet."*

Louis XIV, who was king at this time (it is 1667), was displeased that one so well born should dabble so far below his station. So he, disingenuously, made his cousin a Cardinal. Cardinals may carry on, but not marry.

So Louis de Mercœur, Duke of Vendôme, exchanged his plot on the *Cours* where the rays from the *Roi Soleil* would have warmed him, for his land in the parish of the Franciscans (Cordeliers). He lavished on it his fortune, and he wrote there a sonnet in stone and flowers, a monument to his love, and the pride of Aix's proud palaces. There he died two short years later. *"Las machouettos an tua lou duc"* (The owls have killed the Grand Duke !) For Lucrèce de Rascas, née Forbin Soliès, would enter at night, in disguise, with her servants, all caped and trussed... like night owls.

Two hundred paces away, to the north east on what is now called *avenue Pasteur*, stands another monument, a tribute to Reason, to Justice, and to Joseph Sec, a timber merchant, who, just after the Revolution erected it in 1792. Alone, on the highest pedestal, stands Justice. She carries a pair of scales in her left hand and she is looking stonily, but straight, at the *Pavillon Vendôme*.

94

95

Does she never feel a pang ? Will she one day drop her scales and cross the *traverse de la Mole* to where the *machouettos* entered ?

99

ILLUSTRATIONS

Front cover : Door knocker / back cover : View of the cathedral's steeple, Place de l'Université.
1. Mascaron. 2. Palais de Justice, statue of the comte de Mirabeau. 3. Palais de Justice, Salle des pas perdus. 4. The steps to the Palais de Justice. 5. Church of La Madeleine. 6, 7, 8. Flea market, Place de Verdun. 9, 10. Rue Constantin and the Chapelle de la Visitation. 11. Chapelle du collège des Jésuites. 12. Fountain, rue de la Mule Noire. 13. Mascaron. 14. Rue Espariat. 15. Hôtel de Boyer d'Eguilles. 16, 17. Place d'Albertas. 18, 19. Door and garden of the Hôtel d'Albertas. 20. Sundial, Place Richelme. 21, 22. Market. 23. Telamon, Hôtel d'Arbaud. 24. Hôtel de Ville and Clock Tower. 25 à 28. Flower market. 29, 30. Hôtel de Ville : courtyard and statue of Maréchal-duc de Villars. 31. Place des Cardeurs. 32. Fountain, Place de l'Hôtel de Ville. 33. Gargoyles. 34. Entrance to the cathedral Saint-Sauveur. 35, 36. Baptistery. 37. Cloister. 38, 39. Sculpted capitals. 40. Saint-Pierre. 41. The dome in the baptistery. 42. Hôtel de Maynier d'Oppède. 43. Place de l'Université. 44. Place de l'Archevêché. 45. Interior courtyard of the Hôtel de Ch. de Grimaldi-Régusse. 46. Interior courtyard of the Hôtel de Maynier d'Oppède, before a concert. 47. Door of the Archbishop's palace. 48 to 51. Mascarons. 52. An evening at the Opera Festival. 53. Concert in the cathedral Saint-Sauveur. 54. Fountain, Place de l'Archevêché. 55. Telamon, Hôtel de Maurel de Pontevès. 56. Hôtel d'Arbaud. 57, 58. "Deux Garçons" café. 59. Cafés on the Cours Mirabeau. 60 to 63. The Cours Mirabeau. 64. An "Aixoise". 65. The "left bank" of the Cours Mirabeau. 66, 67. The "Foire aux Croûtes". 68. Statue of the Roi René and the Hôtel du Poët. 69. The Three Graces. 70 to 76. The fountain at the Rotonde. 77. Mascaron. 78, 80. Fountain of the Four Dolphins. 79. Hôtel de Boisgelin. 81. The Saint-Jean-de-Malte fountain and the Musée Granet. 82. Rue Cardinale. 83. Rue Roux-Alphéran, Hôtel de Castillon. 84 to 87. Mascarons. 88. Door knocker. 89. Hôtel de Chateaurenard, "trompe l'œil". 90, 91. Hôtel de Caumont (academy of music). 92. Hôtel Ricard de Saint-Albin. 93. Telamon of the Pavillon Vendôme. 94, 95. Garden of the Pavillon Vendôme. 96. Pavillon Vendôme. 97, 98. Garden and fountain of the Hôtel Maurel de Pontevès. 99. Door knocker.

Achevé d'imprimer le 28 juin 1988
sur les presses de l'imprimerie Intergraphie
42000 Saint-Etienne
Dépôt légal : 3e trimestre 1988

Imprimé en France